MY OLD
Kentucky
ROAD TRIP

★

PRESIDENTS, BATTLES, AND MUST-SEE CIVIL WAR DESTINATIONS

EXPLORING A KENTUCKY DIVIDED

CAMERON M. LUDWICK

&

BLAIR THOMAS HESS

Photography by ELLIOTT HESS

INDIANA UNIVERSITY PRESS

This book is a publication of

Indiana University Press
Office of Scholarly Publishing
Herman B Wells Library 350
1320 East 10th Street
Bloomington, Indiana 47405 USA

iupress.indiana.edu

The paper used in this publication meets the minimum
requirements of the American National Standard
for Information Sciences—Permanence of Paper for
Printed Library Materials, ANSI Z39.48-1992.

Manufactured in the United States of America

Cataloging information is available from the Library of Congress.

ISBN 978-0-253-03897-5 (hardback)
ISBN 978-0-253-03896-8 (paperback)
ISBN 978-0-253-03900-2 (ebook)

1 2 3 4 5   24 23 22 21 20 19

All photos by Elliott Hess unless otherwise noted,
www.elliotthess.com.

*For those who don't shy away
from history and those who follow
the wisdom of Abraham Lincoln
and "must have Kentucky."*

Contents

Acknowledgments

It started with unusual monuments.

When one of us was living in Nashville and the other lived in Lexington, we would try to meet in the middle as often as we could spare the weekend. Our first trip to Mammoth Cave took one of us past the neoclassical, kind of Parthenon-esque Lincoln's Birthplace National Park, and the other past the 351-foot only-thing-in-the-skyline Jefferson Davis Monument. Both monuments wound up on the itinerary pretty quickly, and when the—shall we say—geekier of us took the team to their first reenactment in Perryville, we knew we had to dive into Kentucky's Civil War history.

This book would not be what it is without our intrepid photographer, Elliott Hess. While he wasn't quite fast enough to snag that shot of a young soldier resting against a tree with his rifle in one hand and his cell phone in the other, he did capture the gorgeous photos you're treated to here. From portraits to landscapes and the heat of battle, Elliott's photos are worth more than a thousand words and far more than the thanks we offer him here.

To our editor, Ashley Runyon, and the team at Indiana University Press—our eternal thanks for your patience, understanding, and support while we performed our own reenactment of all the things authors probably shouldn't do. Thank you for helping us take My Old Kentucky Road Trip off the parkways and onto the page.

To Alice at Speilburg Literary Agency, words will never be enough to convey our gratitude for your steady guidance, unfailing patience, faith, and, most of all, friendship. We're so glad to have you along for the ride.

We can't say this loudly enough or often enough: thank you to the state employees, park rangers, groundskeepers, and hospitality managers who make every historic site, monument, resort park, tour, museum, and everything around and between such wonderful tributes to Kentucky—her history and her future. And to the historical societies, community groups, genealogists, librarians, researchers, and our fellow writers—may we never stop seeking and never stop sharing the Commonwealth's important stories.

A twenty-one-gun salute to the reenactors who pour their (fake) blood, (very real) sweat, and (maybe sometimes) tears into recreating the battles that shaped our past and continue to shape our present, and for sharing their knowledge and experiences with inquisitive roadtrippers. We raise our canteens to your thorough dedication and unbridled passion.

While we can't confirm that Abraham Lincoln was thinking of the Kentucky State Seal when he proclaimed, "A house divided against itself cannot stand," in his debate against Stephen Douglas in 1858, we know that without our Kentucky home, this great road trip would have never made it out of the garage. To our families keeping the fires going at our original base camp, thank you. We love you.

Lastly, an apology to the littlest roadtripper on the team: we're sorry we made you wear those giant noise-canceling headphones while the guns and canons exploded at the reenactments. We promise—it was for your health and safety and not our own laughs (mostly).

PRESIDENTS, BATTLES, AND MUST-SEE CIVIL WAR DESTINATIONS

Introduction

My Old Kentucky Road Trip is an ode to our home state. It's a labor of love and a journey to connect with all its parts and all its history—the good and the difficult.

If you haven't already guessed—it's not obvious *at all*—the name of our website and our books is inspired by Stephen Collins Foster's "My Old Kentucky Home," another ode to the Commonwealth. When Foster visited his family at Federal Hill in Bardstown, Kentucky, in the mid-1800s, he was struck not only by the lush, rolling green hills, the meadow in the bloom, and the birds making music all the day but also by the people. All its people.

Most Kentuckians are probably familiar with the controversy surrounding the original lyrics to "My Old Kentucky Home," but few recognize its history as an antislavery ballad. Foster's original lyrics were inspired by Harriet Beecher Stowe's recently published abolitionist novel, *Uncle Tom's Cabin*. Stowe, by the way, based her main character on Josiah Henson, who was owned by the Riley family in Daviess County, Kentucky.

The full original text of "My Old Kentucky Home," though it uses what we recognize today as insensitive and demeaning language, tells the story of a slave who has been sold to the deeper South, where he laments, "The head must bow and the back will have to bend . . . In the field where the sugar-canes grow." Foster's song—which quickly became a hit when it was released in 1853—brought attention to the abolitionist movement. Frederick Douglass even promoted the tune.

The song was taken up by soldiers and their families on both sides of the Civil War. According to My Old Kentucky Home State Park, soldiers would visit Federal Hill during the war and after, in homage to the song's sentimental longing for a home far away. Tourists continued to visit My Old Kentucky Home at Federal Hill, and roughly 150 years later, two Kentucky ladies on a road trip visited too.

It can be easy to brush over the difficult parts of history or to pretend they never happened. Our country still struggles with the consequences and legacy of the Civil War. For our small part as citizens of the Commonwealth, this is our "Old Kentucky Home," and the best way we know to discover our history and what has brought us to the Kentucky of today is to take a road trip.

1 | **The Presidents**

Perhaps Kentucky's biggest distinction in the Civil War was its connection to both the president of the United States of America and the president of the Confederate States of America. Abraham Lincoln and Jefferson Davis were born 254 days and one hundred miles apart, and it's hardly to be believed that Kentucky rooted both of them. For almost three years—until the Davis family moved to Louisiana—Abraham and Jefferson lived within a few days' ride from one another. More than two hundred years later, it only takes about two hours by car to visit the birthplaces of the leaders of the American Civil War.

And those weren't the only similarities between the two—both were youngest sons (though Lincoln did have a younger brother who died in infancy) of farmers who had moved to Kentucky seeking better fortunes, and both had humble origins from birth in a log cabin. But it was when both families had moved from the Bluegrass State that the divide began to widen. The Davises, moderately better situated, moved to the deeper South, and Jefferson grew up well educated on his oldest brother's cotton plantations. The Lincolns, by contrast, headed north to Indiana and Illinois, where Abraham took charge of his own education. Some primary sources and scholars have speculated that the future sixteenth president spent so much of his time reading and studying because he was avoiding difficult farm work and hard labor.

Both future presidents may have left the Bluegrass State as children, but Lincoln found his heart there again when he married Lexington native Mary Ann Todd. Lexington is also home to Transylvania University, where Jefferson Davis studied for a time, which sits on Gratz Park, the site of Mary Todd Lincoln's finishing school and the home of John Hunt Morgan, also known as the Thunderbolt of the Confederacy.

Purposeful roadtrippers will want to save a few days to visit all the sites, but if you're looking for a whirlwind tour, you only need four hours to travel between all three locations!

★ A ROAD TRIP TO HODGENVILLE TO VISIT THE LINCOLNS ★

Abraham Lincoln, born February 12, 1809, at Sinking Spring Farm near Hodgenville, may have moved from Kentucky at seven years old, but his birthplace continued to play a role throughout his life and career. Sorry, Illinois—you may call yourselves the Land of Lincoln, but Kentucky keeps his soul close.

When the cornerstone of the Abraham Lincoln Birthplace National Park was laid by President Theodore Roosevelt in 1909—on Abe's one hundredth birthday—it was a celebration worthy of worldwide attention. The Lincoln Farm Association raised funds to purchase the land along the Nolin River. The group, which included writers Samuel Clemens (Mark Twain) and Ida Mae Tarbell; Samuel Gompers, founder of the American Federation of Labor; presidential candidates William H. Taft and William Jennings Bryan; and editor Henry Watterson of the *Louisville Courier-Journal*, collected more than $350,000 in donations from the American public to purchase the land. Donations were sent from all over in amounts as low as twenty-five cents for what was to be the *first* memorial to Abe. By the time the building was dedicated in 1911, candidate Taft had become President Taft, and he traveled to Hodgenville to officially open the memorial.

Let's clarify a few things first. The national park includes both the Lincoln Memorial Building and the "birth cabin" inside. The park also contains Sinking Spring, Lincoln's boyhood home at

Kentucky honors the birthplace of the sixteenth president of the United States, just a few miles outside of Hodgenville at Sinking Spring Farm. The Abraham Lincoln Birthplace National Park opened in 1909. This monument houses a replica of the cabin where Lincoln was born.

Knob Creek, and the Boundary Oak, an old survey marker that was a landmark in Lincoln's memory.

When you visit the park, the memorial building is the first thing you'll notice. Perched atop a grand hill above Sinking Spring, the memorial was designed to resemble a neoclassical Greek temple. To look inside, you climb fifty-six steps—one for each year of the president's life. In honor of the sixteenth president, the building is surrounded by sixteen columns and features sixteen windows and sixteen rosettes in the ceiling.

Inside, you'll find the symbolic cabin where Abraham Lincoln was born. We say *symbolic* because, well, it's not *actually* Lincoln's birthplace. When the National Park Service took over management of the park, they began to investigate whether or not there was *any* part of the cabin that might have been Lincoln's home.

A historic replica of the cabin where Abraham Lincoln was born to Nancy and Thomas Lincoln on February 12, 1809, at Sinking Spring Farm near Hodgenville, Kentucky. This cabin sits inside the memorial building and could contain some wood from the original cabin.

The popular press even took part in the speculation and investigation of the national controversy.

As it happened, in 1895 a New York entrepreneur purchased land nearby that included *a* cabin. That cabin, which he had intended to become a tourist attraction promoted as Lincoln's birthplace, was sent to Tennessee for the Centennial Exposition in 1897—the same exposition for which the Parthenon was built in Nashville. At the event, the so-called Lincoln cabin was shown next to another log cabin that had reportedly belonged to Jefferson Davis's family. Both were then sent to fairs in Buffalo, New York, Coney Island, and Long Island; afterward, the logs were in a jumbled mess. Eventually, the Lincoln Farm Association purchased the logs to bring them back to the memorial site. When the controversy about the cabins' origins finally hit in 1948, the National Park Service could only conclude that there was no firm evidence to suggest that the cabin had been the real home where Lincoln was born. It wasn't until 2004 that a team from the University of Tennessee dated the logs—which turned out to be thirty-nine years younger than Abraham Lincoln himself.

★ IF YOU GO

- The path to the memorial building and Sinking Spring is wheelchair accessible, but unfortunately, Lincoln's boyhood home sits on a fairly large acreage and is not wheelchair accessible. Additionally, the on-site buildings are not open to the public—though still worth the visit if only for a walk around the original land of Lincolns!
- Leave yourself enough time to explore the visitor center and sign the guest book. We signed our names near several travelers who had come all the way from New Zealand . . . see if you can spot us! The center also includes a museum with artifacts, educational displays, and a really fascinating documentary.
- Chat with the park rangers. Some of our favorite conversations with folks on our trips have been with NPS staff and rangers. This is an especially useful tip if, like us, you find yourself pulling up to the memorial with less than half an hour before closing time.
- Speaking of closing time, check your watch. We showed up almost too late and missed a chance to explore on our first visit because we were coming from the central time zone. The national park itself is in the eastern time zone. Hodgenville, in LaRue County, is where the time zone changes!

Other Monuments to Abe in Kentucky:

- Downtown Hodgenville—Make a stop in the center of town, where Adolph Alexander Weinman's six-foot-tall sculpture of Lincoln sits. When the Hodgenville statue

Presidents at the Lincoln Birthplace

Five US presidents have visited Lincoln's birthplace in Hodgenville: Theodore Roosevelt, to lay the cornerstone; William H. Taft, to dedicate the memorial; Woodrow Wilson, to receive the cabin, memorial building, and land as a gift to the United States from the original Lincoln Farm Association; the *other* Roosevelt, Franklin D., in 1936 for Flag Day; and Dwight D. Eisenhower, who spoke to a crowd of more than eight thousand people at the site in 1954.

was dedicated in 1909, Abraham Lincoln's son, Robert Todd, was in attendance.

- Frankfort—One of the most visited statues of Lincoln in Kentucky stands in the capitol rotunda and was also sculpted by Weinman. The statue was officially unveiled by President William H. Taft when he visited the state to dedicate the Lincoln Birthplace Memorial Building. Other statues in the rotunda include Henry Clay, a personal hero of Lincoln's, and Jefferson Davis.
- Springfield—Because of land and rent issues, the Lincoln family lived in several different places in Kentucky. The Lincoln Legacy Museum and Lincoln Homestead State Park in Springfield commemorate the family's connections to the area and honor Abraham Lincoln's life and career. While you're in town, make a stop at the Mordecai Lincoln House. Mordecai was Abraham's uncle, and because it's a small, small world, Mordecai's wife was a cousin of Samuel Mudd, the doctor who treated John Wilkes Booth's broken leg after he leaped to the stage of Ford's Theater after shooting the president.
- Lexington—Eduardo Kobra's mural on the back wall of the Kentucky Theatre on Main Street is probably the world's most colorful commemoration of Abraham Lincoln. The Brazilian street artist completed the sixty-foot mural in 2013 as part of Lexington's annual

Internationally known Brazilian artist Eduardo Kobra completed a colorful mural on the sixty-foot-tall back wall of the Kentucky Theatre building in downtown Lexington in 2013. The mural is the artist's interpretation of an iconic image of the president from the nineteenth century, the same one that was used to sculpt President Lincoln inside the Lincoln Memorial in Washington, DC.

PRHBTN street art festival. For the best view, pull into the city parking lot on Water Street or the Lextran bus terminal parking garage.

- Louisville—In our irreverent moments, we (lovingly) refer to the Lincoln Memorial at Louisville's Waterfront Park as the "Babe-raham" Lincoln Memorial. The four bas relief sculptures at the park depict important scenes of Lincoln's life, including a shirtless president chopping wood. Snap a selfie with Lincoln's seated statue. If you've just graduated law school, you might make this a stop for graduation photos—Lincoln sits overlooking the water with an open law book in hand.

You can go on a driving tour of Lincoln murals in Louisville as well. Stop for selfies at Kentucky Mount Rushmore on Bardstown Road (also featuring

Muhammad Ali, Colonel Sanders, and Secretariat), and swing by the Bon Air Neighborhood Association mural near historic Farmington.

- Lincoln Heritage Trail—The official Kentucky Lincoln Heritage Trail includes more than twenty-one sites across the state that honor or are related to Lincoln and his legacy. Along with the national and state parks and monuments listed above, the trail includes sites connected to Lincoln's friends and family, such as historic Farmington in Louisville, home to Abe's law partner, Joshua Speed.

★ A ROAD TRIP TO LEXINGTON TO VISIT THE TODDS ★

When Steven Spielberg's Oscar-winning movie *Lincoln* premiered, the first lady made her way to Lexington for an interview at the Mary Todd Lincoln House. And by *first lady*, we do mean first lady of the screen, Ms. Sally Field, who portrayed Mary Todd Lincoln in the film. Field actually made multiple visits to the home, researching her role and working to understand the life of the Lexingtonian.

Situated on Main Street practically next door to Rupp Arena (which some might consider prominent in its own right . . . we have no idea why), the building was, yes, home to the Todd family but, for a time, also home to a well-known brothel. Legal disputes after Mary Todd's father's death led to a public auction and the contents of the home and the home itself being sold off. The residence also served as a boardinghouse and a grocery store.

Belle Brezing, the infamous Lexington madam who was the basis for Belle Watling's character in the movie *Gone with the Wind*, lived in the bawdy house early in her career, working for a madam named Jenny Hill. Belle later went into business for herself and ran houses near Transylvania University—one of which is now a university locker room—and, later, the original Kentucky Association thoroughbred racetrack. Her last brothel

Situated on Main Street in Lexington, this house was home to the Todd family and was where Mary Todd Lincoln, the wife of President Abraham Lincoln, grew up.

ceased operating during World War I because of complaints that it was a distraction to enlisted men, though Brezing continued to live there until her death in 1940.

But enough about brothels. Just as Lincoln's birthplace was the first memorial to the president, the Mary Todd Lincoln House was the first restoration undertaken to honor a former first lady. Though troubled throughout her adult life—crippled by migraine headaches and dramatic mood swings that some scholars have speculated were symptoms of bipolar disorder—Mary Todd was a partner and important influence on her husband. The sixteenth president and his wife were a love match, though the Todds disapproved of their daughter marrying a poor man who came from such humble origins.

After their marriage, however, the Lincolns visited Mary's family in Lexington several times. Lincoln, who was a great fan of Henry Clay, may have met with the Great Compromiser at his

Ashland estate in Lexington. During the Civil War, many of the Todds—especially those who stayed in Lexington—found a few more reasons to dislike Abraham Lincoln. Of the fourteen Todd children, eight supported the Confederacy, and four of Mary's brothers fought for the CSA.

Mary Todd was a staunch abolitionist and outspoken political supporter of her husband, despite being from a city where Lincoln only received two votes in the 1860 presidential election. Yes, you read that correctly—Abraham Lincoln received exactly two votes in Lexington and came in fourth overall in Kentucky. But don't worry; it worked out OK for him in the national election. As Lincoln's political ambitions grew, Mary Todd was never shy about speaking out on her husband's political platform, either in the press or at society functions, and was nicknamed "the hellcat."

Washington society was never quite sure what to do with Mary Todd Lincoln, and many thought her unrefined and too "western." In addition, her family's divided loyalties made some believe that she was actually a supporter of the Confederacy. She was often the center of controversy in the press and in social gossip throughout her husband's presidency—and beyond.

Mary Todd was devastated after his death; she had been holding her husband's hand when he was shot at Ford's Theatre in 1865. That, combined with the overwhelming loss of her eleven-year-old son, Willie, during the war, caused Mary Todd's mental health to break down. She spent her later years struggling with mental illness, and at one point her son Robert Todd had her involuntarily committed to an institution. Ultimately, she lived out her days back in Springfield, Illinois, with her sister, Elizabeth.

★ IF YOU GO

- Pay attention to the decor. Most of the furnishings are the original property of the Todds. When Mary's father, Robert, passed away, the house was opened for auction. The catalog from that auction was used by the restoration committee to help refurnish the house. Many items have also been donated back to the home by their new owners.

- Get ready to walk. The Mary Todd Lincoln House, with assistance from the Bluegrass Trust, has put together a walking tour of downtown Lexington that features sites and stories from both Mary's and Abraham's lives. Within walking distance of the Mary Todd Lincoln House are the home of Mary's maternal grandmother, the original Lexington post office, Henry Clay's law office, Mary's finishing school at Gratz Park, the abolitionist Cassius Clay's newspaper office, and even a building that housed a confectionary said to be the source of Mary's white almond cake recipe.
- Tours of the garden are self-guided, but you'll need a ticket and a docent to see the interior. The tour lasts around an hour, and they do offer discounts for military personnel. Because it is an antebellum home, the upstairs is not wheelchair accessible, but the remainder of the home is.
- Go for a drink at the nearby Belle's Cocktail House, and raise a glass to the portrait of the Mary Todd Lincoln House's *other* famous resident.

★ A ROAD TRIP TO FAIRVIEW, BIRTHPLACE OF THE *OTHER* FIRST PRESIDENT ★

The 555-foot-tall Washington Monument was opened in 1888 and was built to honor the first president of the United States. The 351-foot-tall Jefferson Davis Monument in Fairview, Kentucky, began construction in 1917 and was built to honor the first and only president of the Confederacy. We'll do the math for you—that's two-thirds the size of the Washington Monument!

The *massive* concrete obelisk stands perfectly atop the border of Todd and Christian Counties, near Jefferson Davis's birthplace.

This 351-foot-tall obelisk stands atop the border of Todd and Christian Counties in western Kentucky. The monument opened in 1924 and remains the tallest freestanding concrete structure in the country.

Worth a stop on your way to or from the Land Between the Lakes in Western Kentucky, it's difficult to miss. As you cruise down US 68 just east of Hopkinsville, the monument rises into the clear blue sky just off the highway.

The building of the monument was undertaken by the Confederate Orphan Brigade and initially proposed by Confederate General Simon Bolivar Buckner. When the project ran out of funding after costs skyrocketed following World War I, the United Daughters of the Confederacy raised money to complete construction. The monument was finally dedicated and absorbed by the Kentucky State Parks system in 1924. The monument remains the tallest freestanding concrete structure in the country and is one of the tallest monuments in the United States—in contrast, the Washington Monument is made of marble and granite and is the tallest stone structure in the world.

Davis, in fact, only lived in Kentucky for the first three years of his life, until his family moved to Louisiana and, later,

Mississippi. However, he returned to Lexington in 1821 to attend school at Transylvania College. A historical marker stands on High Street in town, outside the house where he rented a room while at school. The home was owned by Lexington's postmaster—who also happened to be close with Mary Todd Lincoln's family.

The home that the Davis family may have lived in in Fairview, Kentucky, no longer remains. *Supposedly*, the log cabin where Jefferson Davis was born was purchased and went on tour with the alleged Lincoln family cabin in the late nineteenth century. All that remains of Davis's family connection is the memorial, visitor center, and museum at Fairview.

The story of Jefferson Davis and his legacy remains controversial. In Kentucky, there are several monuments to Davis that have incited controversy and community discussion. The most public of these debates has centered around the statue and commemorative plaque of Davis that stands in the capitol rotunda in Frankfort, just behind the statue of Abraham Lincoln. In October 2017, the Kentucky Historic Properties Advisory Commission voted to remove the plaque beneath Davis's statue that read: *Patriot – Hero – Statesman*. A smaller plaque that displays his name, birthday, place of birth in Fairview, and the statement *Only President of the Confederacy* remains. Kentucky, along with Florida, is one of two states that marks Jefferson Davis's June 3 birthday as a public holiday. You might have heard it referred to as Confederate Memorial Day, though future state legislation may remove the state's legal recognition of the holiday, as well as a January 19 observance of Confederate General Robert E. Lee's birthday.

★ IF YOU GO

- The monument is an easy stop to make while you're in western Kentucky. As great fans of the Kentucky state parks (and their lodges), we've passed the Jefferson Davis Monument more than a few times on trips to Lake Barkley Lodge and the Land Between the Lakes.

- The state historic site where the monument sits is absolutely free to visit, but if you want to ride the elevator to the top—and you should, because the view is amazing—you'll have to visit the museum and visitor center to purchase a ticket. As you ride the elevator all the way up, pay attention to the elevator's mechanism; it was originally steam powered!
- Bring your hiking gear. One of the easiest landmarks to spot from the top of the monument is nearby Pilot Rock, a formerly popular local climbing spot. Though Pilot Rock sits on private property now and is not open for climbing, there are plenty of great trails in the area, including lots of rail trails.

2 | **The Battles**

We know Kentucky is special. And you know Kentucky is special—why else would you be reading a book about road trips in Kentucky? And at the outset of the Civil War and the secession crisis, a lot of important people thought that Kentucky was *extra* special.

A strategic territory for both the Union and Confederate states, Kentucky was a prize desired by both President Abraham Lincoln and Jefferson Davis. In an 1861 letter, a few months after the attack on Fort Sumter, Lincoln stated, "I think to lose Kentucky is nearly the same as to lose the whole game."

When you're talking about the Civil War—brother against brother, divided loyalties, and ideological debates—nowhere is that conversation more prominent than in the Bluegrass State. At the start of the war, Kentucky had a Unionist legislature and a Confederacy-sympathetic governor; the western Jackson Purchase region wanted to secede, and the populace had elected nine supporters of the Union and one supporter of the Confederacy to the US House of Representatives.

For the Confederate army, Kentucky's location—abutting the Ohio and Mississippi Rivers—was everything, and Confederate incursions sought to take ground as well as hinder the Union's ability to ship supplies and troops across the country. In addition, the CSA thought that an aggressive strategy and success in border states such as Kentucky and Missouri would bring support from potential allies in Europe, who might see victories as proof of Confederacy's ability to govern their own nation.

For the Union, Kentucky's geography was important strategically, but it was also an important bulwark against the secessionists' ideology. Kentucky sat squarely in the middle of America's differing opinions on slavery. Lincoln thought that if Kentucky were to throw its support to the Confederacy, Missouri and Maryland would go as well. And then the Union would, as he wrote, "lose the whole game."

Geographically, Kentucky hides behind the Appalachian Mountains and is protected by both the Ohio and Mississippi Rivers. Our state's geography was a benefit to both the North and the South at various times, though both prized the easily navigable waterways and rich natural resources—including our horse industry.

At the time, it wasn't easy to move troops across our landscape, but nowadays, it's much simpler to get around the state to visit some of the locations that proved pivotal to both armies during the Civil War. One of the best-known (and spectacular) ways that Kentucky commemorates its role in the Civil War is through reenactments. There are more than a few reenactment companies in our state that join annual reenactments at Kentucky's historic battle sites, including a mounted cavalry unit that reenacts the raids of John Hunt Morgan.

The best ways to find dates for each year's reenactments are through the Kentucky Department of Travel tourism calendar, the Kentucky State Parks, and the Facebook pages and official websites for the battle sites. There are also a few things you'll want to know before you go.

★ RULES FOR REENACTMENTS ★

1. If you bring it with you, take it with you. Don't leave your trash behind!
2. If you're going to bring children or pets, make sure they're not sensitive to loud noises and other animals. It was

A woman sits in Civil War–era costume on the edge of the battlefield at the
Battle of Sacramento reenactment.

Ladies in full Civil War–era costume stand on the edge of the battlefield at the Battle of Perryville reenactment. In addition to reenacting the battles, historically accurate camps are set up on the battlefields and stay up for the entire weekend. Women and children dress up and reenact their roles in the Civil War battles.

Reenactors march toward the battlefield at the Battle of Perryville reenactment. Perryville is the largest annual reenactment in Kentucky, with around two thousand participants annually.

Soldiers in reenactment costumes line up at the start of the battle at the Battle of Perryville reenactment. Soldiers—and their reenactment counterparts—included men and boys of all ages.

A reenactor sits in full costume at the battle camp at the Battle of Perryville. Historically accurate camps are set up on the battlefields and stay full and active for the entire weekend each year. To help them get into character, reenactors go so far as to leave modern comforts at home, including cell phones and flashlights.

Reenactors representing the Union line up waiting for the battle to begin. The Battle of Sacramento is the largest cavalry reenactment in Kentucky.

Confederate reenactors fire a cannon at the Battle of Sacramento reenactment. Civil War–era cannons and guns are used with fake ammunition in the recreated battles.

A father and son reenactment duo represent the Union army at the Battle of Sacramento in McLean County.

Confederate soldiers take their first shots at the Battle of Richmond reenactment, which takes place just outside of Richmond, Kentucky, at the end of August each year.

Real cannons fire blank ammunition at reenactments so visitors can feel the impact of cannon fire in person. Here, Confederate reenactors load and fire cannons at the Battle of Richmond.

A Union soldier reenactor stands ready to fight at the Battle of Richmond.

Confederate soldiers aim their weapons while fallen comrades lie at their feet at the Battle of Richmond reenactment. Infantries must decide which actors will "die" and how they will fall at the start of each battle so that history is accurately represented.

Reenactors in the Union army stand ready for battle at the Battle of Richmond. Fought August 29–30, 1862, this was the first major battle in the Kentucky Campaign and was won by the Confederate army. Today, the reenactment takes place at the end of August each year on the grounds of the Bluegrass Army Depot, just outside of Richmond, Kentucky.

Chaplain Alan Farley stands in full costume at Civil War Days, held at Columbus-Belmont State Park in Columbus, Kentucky. Farley, who stands in front of the flag of his infantry, attends reenactments across the state. Civil War Days takes place in mid-October each year.

A reenactor cooks lunch at his campsite during Civil War Days at Columbus-Belmont State Park in western Kentucky. In addition to battle reenactments, historically accurate camps are set up along the battlefield, and participants sleep and eat with their infantries.

Camp Nelson National Cemetery is situated
a short distance from Camp Nelson Civil War
Heritage Park, which was established in 1863
as a depot for the Union army during the Civil
War and a major hub for the training of African
American soldiers. Today, the cemetery is open
to all members of the armed forces.

A boy attends the Battle of Sacramento reenactment with his father and takes part in the show. Reenactors pledge not to bring modern amenities, such as cell phones, to events.

the Civil War—there were cannons and guns, and they're not particularly quiet weapons. There will also be plenty of other observers with their children and dogs, and the cavalry comes with horses.

3. Wear sturdy shoes. You'll be visiting farms and fields and will definitely be walking over a lot of rough terrain. Many battle sites were chosen for strategic advantage, meaning hills, valleys, trees, and no paved sidewalks.

4. Be patient and kind. The reenactments are a large community undertaking that require coordination among many people. The troops might not start moving on the dot, or you might have to stand behind someone who arrived earlier. Be cool and enjoy.

5. Visit the living history village. Have you ever looked up what it takes to be a reenactor? Those who volunteer make a *serious* investment of time, money, and passion to put together their character. Many base their battlefield background on an ancestor or an interesting figure from history, and they're not shy about telling stories or sharing artifacts. We've spoken with a "camp doctor" who had a full surgery tent setup, an artillery operator who told us how he transports his company's cannon to reenactments, and a friendly "sheriff" who was passing out period-correct money he had recovered from a recent "bank robbery." So step on up and say hello—you never know who you'll meet.

6. Go on the ghost tour! Though one of us is a cowardly chicken and the other ain't afraid of no ghost, we always have a blast listening to the stories of the battlefield guides who lead ghost tours at the Civil War battle sites. If you enjoy hearing personal stories and getting off the beaten path, ghost tours are a great way to dig into a different perspective, one you won't get from the reenactment itself.

★ A ROAD TRIP TO WESTERN KENTUCKY'S BATTLEFIELDS ★

The Battle of Columbus

The fight that started it all for Kentucky was the fight that started it all for future president Ulysses S. Grant. In the beginning, both the Union and Confederacy respected Kentucky's neutrality, worried that an incursion would drive the state to support the other side. But Kentucky's land at the edge of the Ohio and Mississippi Rivers was too appealing for either army to resist.

First, Confederate general Leonidas K. Polk ordered his troops from Missouri across the Mississippi River to build an outpost in Columbus, Kentucky. He nicknamed the spot the Gibraltar of the West, thanks to its location.

Two days later, Ulysses S. Grant, in one of his first maneuvers of the war, sent his forces to take Paducah to control the mouth of the Tennessee River and the important New Orleans and Ohio Railroad.

Furious, Beriah Magoffin, Kentucky's governor and a supporter of neutrality but also of slaveholders' rights, ordered both sides to withdraw. The state legislature, consisting mostly of Union supporters, passed a resolution ordering only the Confederate troops to leave. Surprise, surprise—this led to a big conflict between the general assembly and the governor. After vetoes and veto overrides, the general assembly had the Union flag raised above the capitol in Frankfort, bringing Kentucky's neutrality to an official end.

Grant and Polk skirmished in western Kentucky in late 1861. Generally, the press billed it as a victory for the Confederacy, as Grant had been the aggressor and withdrew his troops. However, casualties were evenly matched, and neither side gained a real advantage as a result. For Grant, one positive did come out of the battle—he caught the attention of President Abraham Lincoln, who promoted him to major general.

Aside from a great view of the Mississippi River, one of the best reasons to visit Columbus-Belmont State Park is to see Polk's chain.

When General Leonidas K. Polk moved his troops from Missouri to Kentucky, he moved them directly across the river for a reason: his chain. The chain, which had *massive* links that weighed more than twenty pounds apiece and stretched more than a mile across the Mississippi River across pontoon boats, was intended to slow and stop Union river traffic downstream. Unfortunately, the giant chain collapsed under its own weight and was too heavy to be supported against the Mississippi's current.

In 1925, following a landslide, city officials unearthed a large segment of chain as well as the anchor, which weighed several tons! Polk's anchor and chain are still on display at Columbus State Park, as well as Lady Polk, a giant cannon that Polk fired upon Grant's forces.

The Battle of Sacramento

Most often known as Forrest's First Fight in honor of Confederate cavalry commander Nathan Bedford Forrest, the Battle of Sacramento seems a bit like a movie. Here's the scene: A group of Union soldiers stops to water their horses. A local woman who supports the Southern cause reports what she's seen to the young commander, Nathan Bedford Forrest, who was spending the winter holiday with his family near Hopkinsville. Forrest, spoiling for a fight, rides out with his regiment—accompanied by the young woman who brought him news of the enemy, Mollie Morehead—to meet the federal troops. He divides his force into three prongs that circle the unsuspecting adversary and attack with gusto.

Just as dramatically as it began, the Battle of Sacramento became a running battle that continued through the small village of Sacramento and toward the Green River for almost two miles,

Reenactors demonstrate battle formations and weaponry while in original uniforms used at the Battle of Sacramento. This reenactment is the largest cavalry reenactment in Kentucky and takes place in May.

culminating in what was described by one of Forrest's scouts as a "mass of men and horses." Though Forrest, who was a popular hero of the Confederacy, unfortunately went on to become an early leader of the Ku Klux Klan, he was an eager fighter and respected tactician, and US military commanders later adapted his battle strategy for mobile warfare. The strategies he exhibited at the Battle of Sacramento and later in the war have been models for military movements and troop deployment in global conflicts ever since.

★ IF YOU GO ▸

The Battle of Sacramento reenactment is the largest cavalry reenactment in Kentucky. Forrest's First Fight is staged on the original battlefield each year during the third full weekend in May. The community performs the full sequence of battle, from Mollie's ride to the cavalry charge.

The Battle of Munfordville

Also known as the Battle for the Bridge, Munfordville was a fight for control of the strategic Louisville & Nashville Railroad's crossing over the Green River and a Confederate victory. Visit the Hart County Civil War Days each September for a three-day community festival that features a reenactment on Saturday and Sunday.

★ A ROAD TRIP TO EASTERN KENTUCKY'S BATTLEFIELDS ★

The Battles of Camp Wildcat and Mill Springs

The story of the Battles of Camp Wildcat and Mill Springs, in neighboring Laurel and Pulaski Counties, features Confederate brigadier general Felix Zollicoffer.

Zollicoffer and his local troops were tasked with maintaining the CSA's control of pro-Union east Tennessee and preventing the incursion of Union troops from the Cumberland Gap, but not necessarily defending the Cumberland Gap itself. In September of 1861, acting on his own initiative, Zollicoffer stationed his troops in the Cumberland Gap and began attacking, pushing Union forces out of Camp Andrew Johnson near Barbourville. In response, the Union troops established Camp Wildcat at the base of Wildcat Mountain in Laurel County, overlooking the Wilderness Road from the Cumberland Gap—and they brought in reinforcements.

Not knowing that the Union forces beyond the gap were now seven thousand men strong, Zollicoffer overconfidently marched his men into eastern Kentucky. The ensuing Union victory was celebrated by the Northern newspapers—which were looking for positive news following the Union's defeat at the First Battle of Bull Run.

Undeterred by this loss and believing that he could strengthen the CSA's position in eastern Kentucky, Brig. Gen. Zollicoffer marched his men back through the Cumberland Gap and set up his winter headquarters at Mill Springs, near present-day Somerset.

When you look at a list of all the battles of the Civil War, you'll notice something about the dates—very few battles took place in January and February, and for good reason. The cold wreaked havoc on troop health, morale, and guns—which were often family antiques and did *not* work in the cold—not to mention the weather was brutal and unpredictable.

As the Union army marched toward Mill Springs to push the CSA back across the Cumberland River, Zollicoffer brought his men out into the wet, mud, and mist, marching through the night to meet them in the early morning.

Whether it was poor eyesight or just the general confusion of a poorly lit, chaotic battle, Zollicoffer, in his white raincoat, rode out to ask a company of men why they were firing on their own troops. Only they weren't members of the CSA—they were a Union regiment. According to firsthand accounts from the

A sketch of the Battle of Camp Wildcat that occurred on October 21, 1861, outside of Camp Wildcat in present-day Laurel County. This sketch was created during the battle by Alfred E. Matthews, Thirty-First Regiment, Ohio. Middleton, Strobridge & Co., lithographer. Courtesy Library of Congress, Prints and Photographs Division, Washington, DC (LC-DIG-pga-11689 DLC), battle, Union colonel Speed Fry rode out to meet with Zollicoffer, neither realizing the other was an enemy combatant until two Confederate soldiers figured out the mistake and shot at the Union commander.

Zollicoffer's death in the salvo of bullets after his mistake was realized is credited historically to Colonel Fry, though the Union commander never officially claimed it. The death of their leader (and a reportedly drunk major general who should have assumed command) sent the CSA into disarray, and Union forces were able to overwhelm the Southern troops.

Northern newspapers celebrated the significant Union victory at Mill Springs, which, along with the victories at Ivy Mountain and Middle Creek, built momentum toward the Union victory at the Battle of Forts Henry and Donelson and helped to cement federal control over Kentucky.

★ IF YOU GO

- Don't miss a stop at Zollicoffer Park, just south of the Mill Springs Battlefield Visitor Center. It's there you'll find the Zollie Tree, or at least the stump of the Zollie Tree, which was struck by lightning in 1995. The tree is recognized as the site of Felix Zollicoffer's fatal mistake. A Confederate memorial marker is also located in Zollicoffer Park.
- See the cannonball hole preserved in the parlor wall at the Brown-Lanier House in Mill Springs. The antebellum home was used as Zollicoffer's headquarters, and it offers guided tours.
- Pay your respects at the Mill Springs National Cemetery, one of the oldest national cemeteries still operating in the United States. Located at the visitor center and museum, the land for the National Cemetery was donated by the family on whose land the Battle of Mill Springs was fought.
- The Battle of Camp Wildcat reenactment is held annually over three days in October, in the heart of the Daniel

Boone National Forest. Admission is free, though donations for battlefield preservation are accepted.
- Because it occurred in January, the Battle of Mill Springs is not commemorated with a reenactment but with an observance at Zollicoffer Park and a community gathering at the battlefield visitor center.
- Both sites offer living history demonstrations, special events, and ghost tours. In addition, the Mill Springs Battlefield Visitor Center and Museum offers a self-guided driving tour, which we absolutely recommend!

The Big Sandy Expedition and the
Battle of Ivy Mountain

Another of Zollicoffer's goals when he decided to bring his forces into Kentucky was recruitment. The Confederacy believed that there was a silent majority of Southern supporters in Kentucky who only needed to be empowered by the CSA.

The Big Sandy Expedition was a federal campaign to nip that in the bud and reaffirm Union support for eastern Kentucky. Kentuckian William "Bull" Nelson—a large, hot-tempered, former navy lieutenant—was tasked with establishing a new brigade in Maysville.

The sensational Bull Nelson led his brigade in two prongs, securing West Liberty in Morgan County and Hazel Green in Wolfe County before consolidating his forces in Salyersville. Despite an ambush by a Confederate contingent at Ivy Mountain on their way to Pikeville, Nelson's troops' quick response at Ivy Mountain pushed the CSA out of Pikeville and into Virginia, ending the CSA's eastern Kentucky offensive.

★ IF YOU GO

There are no reenactments here, but you can visit the Battle of Ivy Mountain Monument just south of Prestonsburg in Ivel, Kentucky, along US 23.

"Bull Nelson"

Born in Maysville, Bull Nelson started his career with the US Navy and was a member of the first class of midshipmen to attend the US Naval Academy at Annapolis. Soon after Abraham Lincoln's inauguration, Nelson volunteered his services directly to his fellow Kentuckian.

Harnessing Bull's eagerness to be involved, President Lincoln sent him to their home state to report on the mood of its people. Nelson came back with a report of support for the Union and a plan to get weapons into their hands. Lincoln sent Nelson back to Kentucky to help his friend Joshua F. Speed coordinate the distribution of arms to Unionists.

Despite his contributions to the navy and his distinguished service in the Civil War—he saw action at the Battle of Shiloh, the Siege of Corinth, and the Battle of Richmond—Bull is unfortunately best remembered for his murder at the Galt House in Louisville at the hands of one of his fellow Union commanders.

General Jefferson C. Davis (a Union officer, not to be confused with the president of the Confederacy) had been sent to Louisville to report to Nelson. It could be that Bull Nelson disliked everyone from Indiana (reportedly true), or it could be that Nelson's dislike of the Hoosier was personality driven, but whatever it was, it drove Bull Nelson to publicly insult Davis several times. In one instance, Nelson called Davis a "damned puppy," at which point Davis flicked a balled-up wad of paper at his fellow commander in the middle of Union headquarters.

When, at the end of his rope, Davis borrowed a pistol, walked up to Bull Nelson, and fired the gun at his heart, he did not run away from the consequences, though ultimately there were none. Within weeks, Davis was released back into active duty, and though he was never promoted to a rank higher than colonel, he did go on to serve under General William Tecumseh Sherman and was appointed as the first commander of the Department of Alaska.

The Battle of Middle Creek

Also known as "the battle that launched a presidency" and the most significant battle in eastern Kentucky, the Battle of Middle Creek was a major stepping-stone for future president James A. Garfield.

Despite their loss at Ivy Mountain, Confederate commanders were reluctant to give up on eastern Kentucky recruitment, and untested Union colonel James A. Garfield was charged with pushing the Confederate forces back to Virginia again. A teacher in Ohio who was newly admitted to the bar, Garfield was a fervent supporter of President Lincoln and the Union cause.

Though the Union and Confederate forces were evenly matched at Middle Creek near Prestonsburg, Garfield's troop positions deceived the Confederate commander into believing the Union forces appeared larger than they were, prompting a Confederate retreat. Garfield's troops were pursuing the retreating Confederates when federal reinforcements arrived, and the CSA retreated to Virginia.

With eastern Kentucky firmly in Union control for the time being, Garfield was promoted to brigadier general and in command of the only Union force in the region. Though celebrated on the battlefield in the Civil War, Garfield had one of the shortest tenures as president of the United States. He died of infection from a bullet wound in an assassination attempt after only two hundred days in office.

★ IF YOU GO ▶

The Middle Creek National Battlefield Foundation commemorates the anniversary of the battle each January and hosts a reenactment each September. When attending the reenactment in September, be sure to prepare for a full day—they host a "Dark Battle" each evening at dusk. For the especially brave, sign up for their yearly ghost walk, which doesn't start until 10:00 p.m.

Reenactors take to the battlefield at the Battle of Perryville, which was perhaps one of the most significant conflicts to take place in Kentucky during the Civil War. It was the largest battle on Kentucky soil and is the largest reenactment in the state, with around two thousand participants each October.

★ A ROAD TRIP TO PERRYVILLE, THE LARGEST CIVIL WAR BATTLE IN KENTUCKY ★

The Battle of Perryville was a battle for Kentucky itself. The largest battle on Bluegrass soil, and one of the bloodiest of the war, Perryville cemented the Union's control of our border state as well its strategic geography.

Prior to Perryville, Confederate commanders targeted Kentucky for invasion, hoping to expand the Confederacy's border to the Ohio River. Successes in western Kentucky had placed the Commonwealth in the Union's control, but the CSA felt that a major battlefield win in Kentucky would swell their ranks with new recruits and tip the balance of political power.

In early October of 1862, Confederate general Braxton Bragg was in Frankfort, which had been recently captured, to celebrate the inauguration of Kentucky's Confederate governor, Richard Hawes, when he got word that federal troops were converging on his own, pushing them toward Perryville and Harrodsburg. After a hurried inaugural ceremony—during which shots and cannon fire could be heard as Union troops sought to recapture Frankfort—Bragg left Frankfort to rejoin General Leonidas K. Polk, who had been left in charge of the Confederate army.

But why did the armies meet in Perryville, a town of only about three hundred residents at the time? Water. The first shots fired at Perryville were at Doctor's Creek on the morning of October 9. Thirsty Union soldiers had discovered small pools of water, but on approach, they ran into a small group of Confederate soldiers with the same idea, filling canteens at Doctor's Creek while waiting for reinforcements.

Ultimately, the Battle of Perryville was a major strategic win for the North. The Union retained control of a prized border state, and the Confederate army of the Mississippi retreated through the Cumberland Gap.

When you attend the Battle of Perryville reenactment today, you'll want to make sure you bring plenty of water with you. It can get warm and sunny and dry in Kentucky in early October. Modern-day Perryville has lots of helpful folks and bottles of water for sale, but as the Girl Scout motto says, "Be Prepared."

The Perryville reenactment is especially extraordinary because it is one of very few reenactments that takes place on the actual ground where the original battle was fought. In general, the national Civil War Trust, which helps to preserve US battlefield parks, doesn't allow commemorative battles to use conserved land. In 2016, for the first time since the battle in 1862, the Perryville State Historic Site was permitted to use H. P. Bottom's farm to recreate the fight for Bottom's barn.

As the Battle of Perryville was the largest battle on Kentucky soil, it's also the largest reenactment in the state—around two thousand participants take part in the commemoration. You'll want to arrive early to explore the living history camps and on-site museum and to ensure that you have a great view for the reenactment.

★ IF YOU GO

- The Perryville Battlefield State Historic Site sets its dates for the annual commemoration and reenactment up to five years in the future on the first weekend of October. Check their website for a full listing of dates.
- Take some cash. There will be a nominal fee for parking, and you never know what you might find at the Perryville Museum Store. There is also an admission fee, which goes toward preservation and the operation of the state historic site. You'll want to check the official website for rates each year. The park does offer discounts for children and veterans.
- Make time to stop at Merchant's Row in downtown Perryville. The street of shops is home to what might be the oldest pre-Civil War retail stores in the country!

★ JOHN HUNT MORGAN'S ROAD TRIP (BY HORSE) ★

One of the most famous Kentuckians in the Civil War, nicknamed the Thunderbolt of the Confederacy, was Brigadier General John Hunt Morgan. Descended from John Wesley Hunt, a founder of Lexington and one of the first millionaires west of the Allegheny Mountains, John Hunt Morgan had quite a lot to live up to. After he was suspended from Transylvania University in Lexington for dueling with a fraternity brother, Morgan enlisted in the US Army. Later, as political tensions began to rise before the Civil War, Morgan founded his own independent militia known as the Lexington Rifles, who joined him in enlisting in the Confederate army. It would not be the first time that the cavalryman made an independent military move.

John Hunt Morgan actually made four raids into his home state: his first raids in the summer of 1862, capturing trains, horses, and enemy soldiers and recruiting soldiers of his own; his Christmas raid later that year, disrupting Union supply lines after the Battle of Perryville; his best-known raid, the so-called Great Raid of 1863; and his last Kentucky raid in 1864, concentrated near Cynthiana.

When Morgan proposed his Great Raid to CSA general Braxton Bragg, the cavalier was already a famous figure. General Bragg, seeing an opportunity for Morgan to provide a distraction from other Confederate aims, approved the raid but ordered him *not* to cross the Ohio River. But Morgan felt that he could stir up Unionist fears in Ohio and Indiana by bringing his raiders farther north and confessed as much to his friend and confidant Basil Wilson Duke. According to at least one source, Morgan was also inspired by reports that he had lost his edge after his recent marriage. Some have speculated that his raid—well publicized by the press on both sides—was an attempt to reassert his wild reputation.

Morgan's Second Kentucky Cavalry rode more than one thousand miles in forty-six days, charging through Tennessee, Indiana, Kentucky, and Ohio. In Kentucky, Morgan attacked farms, supply depots, and trains from Burkesville to Campbellsville to Lebanon to Bardstown to Brandenburg. The most significant Kentucky skirmish along Morgan's route was the Battle of Tebbs Bend, in which an outnumbered Union force fought off Morgan's attacking cavalry eight times before Morgan acknowledged defeat and withdrew.

After crossing from Kentucky into Indiana and traveling across Indiana into Ohio—where he *wasn't* supposed to be—Morgan made it as far north as Lisbon, Ohio, between Cleveland and Pittsburgh, where he was finally captured. Morgan's raid took him farther north than any other Confederate troops during the entire war, though it was against the direct orders of General Bragg. On their capture, Morgan and his men were taken to the Ohio Penitentiary in Columbus. Most of his cavalry remained there for the rest of the war . . . but not Morgan. In his cavalier style, he and six men tunneled their way out of the prison. Two were recaptured, but Morgan made his way back across the Ohio River and lived to raid again.

★ IF YOU GO

There are a few reenactments of Morgan's exploits in Kentucky:
- Brandenburg, Kentucky, reenacts Morgan's crossing of the Ohio River on even-numbered years in July.
- Cynthiana, Kentucky, celebrates Civil War Weekend each June and reenacts the Second Battle of Cynthiana, Morgan's last engagement in Kentucky.

- Tebbs Bend does not offer a reenactment, but the battlefield is preserved, and the Tebbs Bend Battlefield Association provides a self-guided driving tour of the area as well as access to the Atkinson-Griffin House Museum at the Green River Lake Visitor Center, near Campbellsville.

Morgan's Legendary Kiss

Popular legend in Lexington states that while stopping over in Lexington at some point during the war, Morgan found himself being pursued by Union troops. Wanting to say goodbye to his mother at their family home, Morgan rode his horse into the front entryway, kissed his mother, and continued straight out the back door, jumping over the garden wall to escape his pursuers.

3 | Kentucky War Stories

It took more than four years, more than $5 billion, and more than 750,000 dead, including a beloved president, before the last shots of the Civil War were fired.

The stories of the presidents, the battles, and the victories and losses are, of course, important. But it's also important to remember the lesser-known histories of Kentucky and Kentuckians in the Civil War. We've addressed a few here, but there are many, many more to discover. From Kentucky stops on the Underground Railroad to the Women of the Civil War Museum—the only one of its kind in the world—in Bardstown, don't stop your exploration here.

★ KENTUCKY'S CONFEDERATE CAPITAL ★

The issue of Kentucky's neutrality was one of the most consistent struggles during the Civil War. In an 1861 letter to friend and fellow Kentucky native O. H. Browning, Abraham Lincoln wrote, "I think to lose Kentucky is nearly the same as to lose the whole game," a reference to Kentucky's strategic and cultural importance to the federal war effort.

Just after Lincoln's first inauguration and the outset of the secession crisis, Kentucky was larger (proportionally speaking) than it is today. The influence of its ten seats in the US House of Representatives was desired by both Unionists and secessionists,

Troops under General Leonidas Polk fortified a strategic line of bluffs along the Mississippi River in September 1861, marking the Confederate States of America's first move in Kentucky. These forts are now commemorated at Columbus-Belmont State Park in Columbus, Kentucky.

and neither party wanted to drive the state's voters or legislators to support the other side's cause. In addition, Kentucky was prized for its agricultural and geographic resources. In particular, both factions wanted control of the Ohio and Mississippi Rivers and access to Kentucky's horse industry—because you couldn't fight a war by tank or Humvee in the 1860s.

The combined actions of an eager Confederate general and Ulysses S. Grant lit the fuse that broke Kentucky's neutrality. CSA general Leonidas K. Polk dubbed the border city of Columbus, Kentucky, the Gibraltar of the West, with its position on the Mississippi River. When the position at Columbus—with its view of the river—became too tempting for Polk, he moved his forces across to take a position. Grant responded in kind, moving Union troops into nearby Paducah and taking control of an important railroad that carried shipments to and from New Orleans.

Governor Beriah Magoffin—Kentucky's first Civil War–era governor—ordered both forces to withdraw from the state and from their violation of its neutrality. When neither side complied and a state election in 1861 saw Unionists take a decided majority in both the US House of Representatives and the Kentucky legislature, Governor Magoffin raised the Union flag over Kentucky's capital, Frankfort.

Supporters of the Confederacy in Kentucky—many of them concentrated in the western Jackson Purchase region of the state—formed a shadow government, which, at a convention in Russellville later that year, officially separated themselves from the rest of the state. Kentucky's Confederate government—led by their first elected governor, George W. Johnson, and a council of ten men who acted as a provisional legislature—set up their capital in Bowling Green.

Why Bowling Green? At the time, it was firmly in the control of Confederate general Albert Sidney Johnston, who was Jefferson Davis's most respected commander until his death at the Battle of Shiloh. However, realizing their newly formed government might not have as secure a foothold as they might need during such a tumultuous period, the convention delegates made a provision for the convening of Kentucky's Confederate government to be at any place agreed upon by the governor and elected council. Though Jefferson Davis was concerned by the unusual and secretive formation of the Bluegrass State's secessionist delegation, he admitted Kentucky to the Confederacy in December 1861. Officially, neither Kentucky nor Missouri were ever administrated by Davis's Confederate government. But, when the Confederate States of America adopted their battle flag, Kentucky was represented by the central star of the design.

When General Albert Sidney Johnston eventually moved his troops from Bowling Green, Governor Johnson and his council followed. At the time, the New Orleans newspaper joked that "the capital of Kentucky [is] now being located in a Sibley tent." (In case you were wondering, a Sibley tent is a canvas tent that could house up to a dozen men; it was in popular use during the Civil War.)

For a short time in 1862, Kentucky's Confederate government controlled Frankfort—the only time during the war when a Union capital was captured by Confederate forces. You might recall that CSA general Braxton Bragg was in the recently taken capital city for the inauguration of Kentucky's second (and last) Confederate governor when he was called to meet his army as they clashed with Union forces at Perryville. Reports of the inauguration mention the sound of cannon fire from approaching Union troops on their way to recapture Frankfort. Confederate governor Richard Hawes's planned inauguration ball that evening was canceled, but he continued as Kentucky's confederate governor for the duration of the war.

After their defeat at Perryville, the officials of the Kentucky Confederacy disbanded and spread out to family homes and places where they could support themselves and their families. The provisional government they had formed, which now existed only on paper, did very little in the way of governance in the Commonwealth. The council and CSA had difficulty collecting taxes and recruiting troops. The undeveloped government received most of their financial support from an independently wealthy state congressman. Though they had no true capital and no sitting legislature—or at least not a legislature that sat in a room together—one of the few measures they did pass was a resolution to rename Wayne County for General Felix Zollicoffer, who died at the Battle of Mill Springs. Clearly the name didn't last beyond the war; Wayne County, Kentucky, still exists today.

★ IF YOU GO ▶

Bowling Green and Warren County have put together a fantastic Civil War driving tour of the area. Sites include Lost River Cave, where John Hunt Morgan is said to have hidden during one of his infamous raids; Fort Lytle, on Western Kentucky University's campus; and the Historic Railpark and Train Museum, which features exhibits on the history and importance of the Louisville & Nashville Railroad in Bowling Green.

★ KENTUCKY'S CIVIL WAR GOVERNORS ★

Between the Kentucky state government and provisional Confederate government, Kentucky was led by five governors during the Civil War.

> *Beriah Magoffin* was elected governor in 1859 and saw the state through its neutrality crisis in 1861. Officially, Magoffin neither wanted to secede and rebel nor take away the rights of slaveholders in Kentucky, though privately, he was a secessionist. When voters elected a legislature that was overwhelmingly Unionist, Magoffin struggled to get along with the general assembly. In 1862, Magoffin agreed to resign, but only if he could pick his successor.
>
> *James Fisher Robinson* was Magoffin's choice. He supported the Union but did not want to revoke slaveholders'

rights. It was Robinson who held the office when Confederate forces took Frankfort, and he fled to Louisville as the CSA occupied the capital. Robinson served just over a year as governor—the remainder of Magoffin's term—before Kentucky's twenty-third governor was elected.

Thomas E. Bramlette served the longest term of any Union or Confederate governor of Kentucky during the war. Bramlette's most pressing issue was shepherding Kentucky through the end of slavery, the end of the Civil War, and the beginning of the tumultuous Reconstruction. Kentucky's status as a border state and the divided loyalties of brother against brother made it difficult to mend political and cultural ties among its citizens. Bramlette did not support slavery, but he didn't support legal rights for slaves and former slaves, either. His term as governor actually saw him withdraw his support from President Lincoln and the Union because of Lincoln's decision to recruit African Americans for the Union army. In a dramatic proclamation, Bramlette declared he would "bloodily baptize the state into the Confederacy." Kentucky's final Civil War governor does have one very important and lasting legacy to his tenure—he established the Kentucky Agricultural and Mechanical College in 1865, which became the University of Kentucky.

George W. Johnson was the first Confederate governor of Kentucky. When the new Confederate government of Kentucky was forced from the state after CSA defeats at the Battles of Forts Donelson and Henry, he joined the staff of his cousin and former vice president of the United States, Confederate general John C. Breckinridge. Johnson was killed in action at the Battle of Shiloh. His time as governor of Confederate Kentucky lasted a mere 140 days.

The Thomas D. Clark Center for Kentucky History in Frankfort is a museum and research facility that features live performances, interactive exhibits, and dynamic collections, including extensive records of state history.

Richard Hawes, Kentucky's only other Confederate governor, served almost three years. Prior to his inauguration, Hawes traveled with General Braxton Bragg's army as it invaded Kentucky from Tennessee. After Bragg's defeat at the Battle of Perryville, Hawes left the state for Virginia to lobby Jefferson Davis for another Confederate invasion of Kentucky. When the war ended, Hawes returned to the Bluegrass State and became a judge, though his rulings were not kind to former slaves.

Allow us a moment to thank and appreciate the Kentucky Historical Society's groundbreaking Civil War Governors of Kentucky project. At the time we began researching this book, the KHS initiative had identified more than 23,300 documents of Kentucky's Civil War governors, scanned almost 23,000, and transcribed more than 13,500. The work the KHS is doing to index and make available primary sources and histories of pivotal people, places, and events in our state's history is invaluable. If you've never stopped by the Thomas D. Clark Center for Kentucky History in downtown Frankfort, we don't know what you're waiting for!

The Incongruity of Simon Bolivar Buckner

Buckner was one of Kentucky's great contradictions. He was a West Point graduate who fought in the Mexican-American War and was originally recruited by the Union army. He rejected their commission, joined the CSA, and saw most of his Civil War action in Kentucky. Oddly, though he served the Confederacy, Buckner was great friends with future president and Union general Ulysses S. Grant, whom he had known from West Point and the Mexican-American War. Despite surrendering to Grant at the Battles of Fort Henry and Fort Donelson—the first Confederate general to surrender an army during the war—he paid for and was a pallbearer at Grant's funeral and even provided a pension to Grant's widow until her death.

As unusual as Buckner's Civil War career was, he is maybe best known in the Bluegrass State as Kentucky's thirtieth governor. His tenure as governor, from 1887 to 1891, was even more noteworthy than his military service. During his time in office, Buckner dealt with the infamous Hatfield-McCoy feud and the Rowan County War, was hit with scandal when state treasurer James "Honest Dick" Tate stole $250,000 from the Kentucky Treasury, and vetoed more legislative bills than the previous ten governors combined, a deed for which he was gifted a Veto Hatchet from a local axe-manufacturing company.

★ A ROAD TRIP TO THE *OTHER* FORT BOONESBORO ★

One of Kentucky's most interesting landmarks is Fort Boonesboro. No, not the recreated pioneer-era fort modeled after Daniel Boone's original outpost. *This* Fort Boonesboro,

Located just outside of Nicholasville, minutes away from the Kentucky River, Camp Nelson was the third-largest recruitment and training center for African Americans in the United States. Today, tours are available of the camp and grounds, which were named for Major General William "Bull" Nelson.

almost directly across the river from the larger state park, is an earthworks fortification built high above the Kentucky River and was an important defensive structure for the Union army.

Though not much of the fort remains today—in its time, it was less a fort and more a series of trenches and walls—the hike to the original site is a must-do. But be prepared—it is a hike. The fort was placed in a necessarily difficult-to-access spot, and construction materials and army supplies were hauled up the side of a very steep climb to the top of the palisades.

It was originally built and manned by African American soldiers serving in the Union army; Clark County now maintains the site. It's easy to find on KY-1924 (just off I-75 toward Winchester), thanks to the colorful murals that adorn the roadside parking area and illustrate early life along the Kentucky River. As you make your way up the half-mile (unpaved) hike, you can follow along with the history of the Civil War fort on educational sign posts and even a self-guided cell phone tour. At the top, you'll have an *incredible* view of the Kentucky River and palisades and even that *other* Fort Boonesboro.

★ AFRICAN AMERICAN SOLDIERS IN KENTUCKY DURING THE WAR ★

Despite Governor Bramlette's vehement opposition to African Americans serving in the Union army, more than twenty-three thousand black Kentuckians joined the federal army when it began recruiting in the Bluegrass State in 1864. The USCT (United States Colored Troops) who volunteered from Kentucky made up more than one-third of all Kentucky volunteers to the Union army.

Camp Nelson, just outside of Nicholasville, was the third-largest recruitment and training center for American Americans in the entire country. Many of the soldiers brought their families when they arrived, fleeing slaveholders and seeking opportunities. The military depot struggled to accommodate the women

Green Hill Cemetery in Frankfort was established at the end of the Civil War to honor the African American troops who served. In the early twentieth century, the women of the Kentucky Colored Corps raised funds to build a monument with the names of 142 African American soldiers from Franklin County who fought in the Civil War. The cemetery is located on E. Main Street near the intersection of KY-421.

and children, and eventually the army ordered a refugee camp be established on-site. More than three thousand people established residence in the community created at Camp Nelson, which included education and medical care, provided by the Army and American Missionary Association. One of the most supportive missionaries was the Reverend John G. Fee, a staunch abolitionist who founded Ariel College at Camp Nelson and the nationally acclaimed Berea College—the first interracial and co-educational college in the South.

Today, African American soldiers' contributions to Kentucky during the Civil War are commemorated not only at Fort Boonesboro and Camp Nelson but also with the Kentucky African American Civil War Soldiers' Monument at Green Hill Cemetery in Frankfort. Green Hill Cemetery was established just after the Civil War as the final resting place for the African

American troops who served. In the early twentieth century, the women of the Kentucky Colored Corps, a division of the Women's Relief Corps of the Grand Army of the Republic, raised funds to build a monument with the names of 142 African American soldiers from Franklin County who fought in the Civil War. When the monument was dedicated in 1924, it was one of only four monuments of its kind. There are fewer than fifty monuments dedicated to African American soldiers in the Civil War today—a very small percentage compared to the thousands of Civil War monuments and memorials total.

★ THE WORDS OF THE WAR ★

William Wells Brown

One of Kentucky's greatest—though, unfortunately, less remembered—writers was William Wells Brown, who wrote *Clotel*, published in 1853, the first novel written by an African American. He was also the first published African American playwright and wrote the first history of African Americans in the Revolutionary War.

Brown was born into slavery near Mount Sterling. Though his father, the half brother of his master, did formally claim Brown as a son, he was sold away from his mother, against his father's wishes, and worked on riverboats along the Mississippi River until he escaped to Ohio at age twenty. After his escape, he learned to read and write and worked for a time at a small printing press until he went to England to lecture on abolition and equal rights.

When Brown left the United States for London, he followed in the footsteps of *another* nineteenth-century African American writer you've definitely heard of—Frederick Douglass. Douglass's own fame and writing often overshadowed the Kentuckian's. Brown's first work, *Narrative of William W. Brown, a Fugitive Slave. Written by Himself,* was a best seller, though didn't sell quite as well as *Narrative of the Life of Frederick Douglass.*

Brown built a career for himself overseas as a lecturer and became well known as a travel writer, long before Mark Twain would do the same. His travelogue, *Three Years in Europe: Or, Places I Have Seen and People I Have Met* was widely read.

Brown's most famous work, *Clotel, or, The President's Daughter: A Narrative of Slave Life in the United States*, fictionalized the rumors of Thomas Jefferson's affair with Sally Hemmings and their children together. The tale was scandalous gossip at the time, and *Clotel* was reissued in four separate editions over fifteen years. Though a sensational story—written as a sentimental nineteenth-century novel, typical of its time—Brown's goal with *Clotel* was to represent the institution and horrors of slavery in a way that might penetrate the ideals of nonabolitionists.

The Fugitive Slave Act of 1850 kept Brown in Europe until friends purchased his freedom in the United States—the same friends had also purchased Douglass's freedom. On Brown's return to the United States in 1854, Brown settled in the Northeast and continued to write and lecture on progressive reforms; he went on to open a medical practice in Boston as well. During the Civil War, he not only spoke out on emancipation but helped recruit volunteers for the USCT. Today, you can commemorate William Wells Brown's legacy at the Kentucky Writers Hall of Fame in Lexington, where an elementary school is also named in his honor.

A "True American"

Let's play a game—name this famous Kentuckian: a brawler in well-publicized fights with a fiery spirit and a way with words.

If you guessed Cassius M. Clay, you must know all about the greatest—the greatest nineteenth-century politician and newspaperman, that is. There was, in fact, a young man named Cassius Marcellus Clay who was born in Louisville in 1942 and later changed his name to Muhammad Ali, and you might know that he became a prominent figure in Kentucky and US history. But *this* Cassius Clay was a cousin of the Great Compromiser

Home of Cassius Marcellus Clay, an emancipationist, publisher, and US minister to Russia appointed by President Abraham Lincoln, White Hall is a forty-four-room mansion located in Lexington. It is open for tours Wednesday through Sunday between April and October.

himself and founded the *True American*, an abolitionist newspaper that caught the eye of President Abraham Lincoln.

Clay was born near Richmond, Kentucky, into a slave-owning family, on a plantation. He attended Transylvania and Yale Universities, and it was at Yale where he heard a speech from abolitionist and *Liberator* editor William Lloyd Garrison, which first planted the kernel for Clay's own antislavery beliefs.

Muhammad Ali may be the better-known Kentucky fighter, but Cassius Clay held his own in a confrontation as well. In 1835, Clay was elected to the Kentucky House of Representatives, where his abolitionist views created a lot of enemies. He fended off assassination attempts at the Kentucky Capitol *twice*—once pulling a bowie knife on an attacker who had shot him in the chest.

His life didn't get much easier after his early political service. When he founded the *True American* newspaper in 1845 in

Lexington—a culturally Confederate city—he provisioned his office at Main and Mill Streets like a well-defended garrison. Because of frequent death threats and attacks, Clay kept himself armed and installed two cannons just inside his office, behind his barricaded and defensible doors. It wasn't until a large mob attacked the newspaper and stole Clay's printing equipment that he finally pulled up roots and moved his operation to Cincinnati.

At the start of the Civil War, President Lincoln named Clay US ambassador to Russia, though he was recalled for a time to serve as a major general in the Union army. He returned to Russia as a U.S. minister until 1869. Clay's final contributions included assisting in the United States' purchase of Alaska, supporting an early Cuban independence movement, and helping to secure the nomination of Horace Greeley for president. He never did get rid of the cannons, though. Clay continued to receive threats and became more paranoid as he aged; he kept a cannon installed in both his home and his office. For the rest of his long life—he lived to be ninety-two—he always carried two pistols and his trusted bowie knife.

Useful Links & Further Reading

These are a few of our favorite books, websites, and sources to explore more about the Civil War in Kentucky.

★ GENERAL LINKS ★

Kentucky Historical Society
100 W. Broadway Street
Frankfort, KY 40601
www.history.ky.gov

KHS Civil War Governors of Kentucky
www.civilwargovernors.org

The Filson Historical Society
1310 S. 3rd Street
Louisville, KY 40208
www.filsonhistorical.org

Civil War Trust
www.civilwar.org

Lincoln Heritage Trail
www.abelincoln.tours

★ BATTLEFIELDS ★

Columbus-Belmont State Park
350 Park Road
Columbus, KY 42032
**www.parks.ky.gov/parks/recreationparks
/columbus-belmont**

Camp Wildcat Civil War Battlefield
Old Wilderness Road
East Bernstadt, KY 40729
www.wildcatbattlefield.org

Battle of Ivy Mountain Monument and
    Middle Creek National Battlefield
KY-114
Prestonsburg, KY 41653
Navigate to the intersection of Mountain Parkway (KY-114)
    and State Highway 404. Follow the brown, state historical
    marker signs to the site.
**www.prestonsburgky.org/battlefield;
    www.middlecreek.org/**

Mill Springs Battlefield and Zollicoffer Park
9020 Highway 80
Nancy, KY 42544
www.millsprings.net

John Hunt Morgan's Raids at Cynthiana
www.cynthianabattlefieldsfoundation.org/

Munfordville Battlefield
113 Main Street
Munfordville, KY 42765
www.visitmunfordville.com/CWDs_Home.html

Perryville Battlefield State Historic Site
1825 Battlefield Road
Perryville, KY 40468
www.perryvillebattlefield.org

Battle of Sacramento Driving Tour
218 West 3rd Street
Sacramento, KY 42372
www.battleofsac.com

Tebbs Bend—Green River Bridge Battlefield
2218 Tebbs Bend Road
Campbellsville, KY 42718
www.tebbsbend.org

★ HISTORIC SITES AND MONUMENTS ★

Abraham Lincoln Birthplace National Historical Park
995 Lincoln Farm Road
Hodgenville, KY 42748
www.nps.gov/abli

Jefferson Davis State Historic Site and Monument
258 Pembroke-Fairview Road
Pembroke, Kentucky 42266
www.parks.ky.gov/parks/historicsites/jefferson-davis/

Camp Nelson
6614 Danville Road
Nicholasville, KY 40356
www.campnelson.org

Civil War Driving Tour of Bowling Green and Warren County
352 Three Springs Road
Bowling Green, KY 42104
www.trailsrus.com/civilwar

Hunt-Morgan House
201 North Mill Street
Lexington, KY 40507
www.bluegrasstrust.org

Leslie Morris Park at Fort Hill
400 Clifton Avenue
Frankfort, KY 40601
**www.frankfortparksandrec.com/Parks
/Leslie_Morris/leslie_morris.html**

Mary Todd Lincoln House
578 West Main Street
Lexington, KY 40507
www.mtlhouse.org

★ OTHER PLACES OF INTEREST ★

Ashland: The Henry Clay Estate
120 Sycamore Road
Lexington, KY 40502
www.henryclay.org

Cave Hill Cemetery and Arboretum
701 Baxter Avenue
Louisville, KY 40204
www.cavehillcemetery.com

Farmington Historic Plantation
3033 Bardstown Road
Louisville, KY 40205
www.farmingtonhistoricplantation.org

Frankfort Cemetery
215 East Main Street
Frankfort, KY 40601
www.heritage.ky.gov/kas

Green Hill Cemetery
East Main Street and Atwood Avenue
Frankfort, KY 40601
www.capitalcitymuseum.com/html/green_hill.html

Hardin County History Museum
201 West Dixie Avenue
Elizabethtown, KY 42701
www.hardinkyhistory.org

Kentucky Military History Museum
125 East Main Street
Frankfort, KY 40601
**www.history.ky.gov/portfolio/kentucky-military
-history-museum/**

Kentucky Gateway Museum Center
215 Sutton Street
Maysville, KY 41056
www.kygmc.org

Lexington Cemetery
833 West Main Street
Lexington, KY 40508
www.lexcem.org

Octagon Hall Museum/Kentucky Confederate Studies Archive
6040 Bowling Green Road
Franklin, KY 42134
www.octagonhall.com/octagon/index.html

Pewee Valley Confederate Cemetery and Monument
Maple Avenue between Old Floydsburg Road and
    Cross Brook Drive
Pewee Valley, KY 40056
www.explorekyhistory.ky.gov/items/show/691

Waveland State Historic Site
225 Waveland Museum Lane
Lexington, KY 40514
www.parks.ky.gov/parks/historicsites/waveland/

White Hall State Historic Site
500 White Hall Shrine Road
Richmond, KY 40475
www.parks.ky.gov/parks/historicsites/white-hall/

★ SELECTED BIBLIOGRAPHY ★

Cashon, John Philip. *Paducah and the Civil War*. Charleston, SC: History Press, 2016.

Craig, Berry. *Hidden History of Kentucky in the Civil War*. Charleston, SC: History Press, 2010.

Harrison, Lowell H. *Kentucky's Governors*. Lexington: University Press of Kentucky, 1985.

———. *Lincoln of Kentucky*. Lexington: University Press of Kentucky, 2010.

Harrison, Lowell H., and James C. Klotter. *A New History of Kentucky*. Lexington: University Press of Kentucky, 1997.

Kleber, John E., ed. *The Kentucky Encyclopedia*. Lexington: University Press of Kentucky, 1992.

Klotter, James C., and Freda C. Klotter. *A Concise History of Kentucky*. Lexington: University Press of Kentucky, 2008.

McEuen, Melissa A., and Thomas H. Appleton Jr., eds. *Kentucky Women: Their Lives and Times*. Athens: University of Georgia Press, 2015.

Noe, Kenneth W. *Perryville: This Grand Havoc of Battle*. Lexington: University Press of Kentucky, 2011.

Penn, William A. *Kentucky Rebel Town: The Civil War Battles of Cynthiana and Harrison County*. Lexington: University Press of Kentucky, 2016.

Sanders, Stuart W. *The Battle of Mill Springs, Kentucky*. Charleston, SC: History Press, 2013.

Sears, Richard D. *Camp Nelson, Kentucky: A Civil War History*. Lexington: University Press of Kentucky, 2002.

Thomas, Edison H. *John Hunt Morgan and His Raiders*. Lexington: University Press of Kentucky, 1975.